VINTAGE
TRAILER VOYEUR

A peek inside the unique custom trailer culture

Victoria Ocken

Schiffer Publishing Ltd

4880 Lower Valley Road · Atglen, PA 19310

Library of Congress Control Number: 2016959667

Designed by Brenda McCallum
Type set in Imprint MT / Alys / Archer
ISBN: 978-0-7643-5128-0
Printed in China

Published by Schiffer Publishing, Ltd.
4880 Lower Valley Road | Atglen, PA 19310
Phone: (610) 593-1777; Fax: (610) 593-2002
E-mail: Info@schifferbooks.com | Web: www.schifferbooks.com

Other Schiffer Books on Related Subjects:
Ready to Roll: The Travel Trailer in America, Arrol Gellner & Douglas Keister, ISBN 978-0-7643-4644-6

Camper & RV Humor: The Illustrated Story of Camping Comedy, John Brunkowski & Michael Closen, ISBN 978-0-7643-4705-4

For our complete selection of fine books on this and related subjects, please visit our website at www.schifferbooks.com. You may also write for a free catalog.

Schiffer Publishing's titles are available at special discounts for bulk purchases for sales promotions or premiums. Special editions, including personalized covers, corporate imprints, and excerpts, can be created in large quantities for special needs. For more information, contact the publisher.

We are always looking for people to write books on new and related subjects. If you have an idea for a book, please contact us at proposals@schifferbooks.com.

For my children, who have forgiven me my shortcomings,
and my husband, who always believes I can do anything. They have given me
the opportunity to soar without limitations, travel without boundaries,
laugh every day, and live my life to the fullest.

"If you don't know where you are going, any road can take you there."

—Lewis Carroll, *Alice in Wonderland*

Acknowledgments

Thank you to the countless people who opened up their hearts and told me their stories.
Their passion and dedication to vintage trailers knows no bounds. They come from all walks of life
and are motivated by many different things, but all have found a connection with the past.
Without them, this book would not have been possible.

CONTENTS

The 1950s trailer on the ranch where I was abandoned and ultimately saved.

INTRODUCTION

Everyone has a story. My story has been intertwined with trailers from an early age when I was abandoned in one as an infant. Swaddled tightly so I couldn't learn to walk, I was rescued by a seven-year-old girl who stepped in when others feared to intervene. Safe with my new family, I ultimately spent my childhood running wild and free, with summers at the lake camping in a converted school bus. This was the one place I felt safe, nestled under the table in the special bed made just for me. It was the only place I didn't have the dreams that terrorized and haunted me nightly. I spent half my life trying to escape those memories and the ghosts that chased me, and now it seems that in the other half of my life, I might be trying to go back.

As an adult, I clawed my way to success, always out-working the other person so I didn't have to go back to living in the trailer of my very early childhood or in the trailer park where I spent time as a young adult. I wanted the American dream: the big house, multiple cars, and a house full of possessions. Many years later, even after I had all this and more, I found myself inexplicably drawn to old trailers, craving the security and solitude they offered. They beckon me, giving me assurance that I will be secure and sheltered. That they will give me a place to call home no matter what life has in store. I feel safe wrapped in their old skins and want to give them a chance to be loved again, to avoid rotting in fields along forgotten roads or languishing in junkyards waiting to be sold for scrap. I have an affinity for the smell of old wood, the sound of rain on tin, and the small spaces they offer. I see the unique soul each has to offer and feel the past lives they have led.

The smallest link to the past thrills me. Forgotten mementos of trips taken long ago—a stray spoon or cup, map, or old manual. The minutest tokens of the past are carefully stored, to be returned to their rightful place when it is time. It is important to me to keep the past intact while living in the present. Much like me, the past is what has made these trailers what they are today. I cherish every dent, scratch, and wrinkle. I like the feel of their old linoleum under my bare feet, the soft glow of varnished birch, and the simplicity of design. They are perfect to me. Bringing them back to life and spending time in them brings me a special kind of joy, but I am not alone in this quest.

When do you have too many trailers, and where do you stop? I will let you know when I get there, but for now, each trailer speaks to me in a different way. That is my story. Many others join me in telling theirs.

A vintage, unrestored Kompac Sportsman camper trailer and boat displayed
at the Pismo Beach Vintage Trailer Rally. It has a certain charm just as it is, a life story filled with
adventures we can only guess at. I wouldn't change a thing.

Chapter One

The perfect trailer—Restorations

The people who restore old trailers are a special group. Constantly on the lookout for treasures behind buildings, in alleys, fields, or on the Internet, they each have their own motivation. Some like to tear them down to the frame and rebuild them better than before, with every modern convenience, while others wouldn't dream of altering the past. They see the romance that lies in old trailers waiting to be rejuvenated. They want them just as they were. These folks do share a common bond: the excitement and pure joy when they find that old trailer and bring it home. They look past the dirt, grime, rust, and smell that years of neglect have bequeathed on these beauties. They only see the possibilities and immediately start plotting the resurrection and the places they will go when the renovation is done. Crumbled walls, rusted frames, and missing parts are overlooked because they know they can rebuild and restore. They show up with duct tape, rope, and tires, and drag their prizes home.

Finding the elusive trailer to restore is half the fun as they scour junkyards, Craigslist, and the extensive resources they have built over the years. They feel the tingle of anticipation run up their spine as they sort through the past, thrilled with the slightest piece of memorabilia. A postcard, original upholstery hidden under slipcovers, or a forgotten toy—anything that tells a tale of the past and the ghosts that lurk there. They replace screws with period fasteners, search for glass lenses for taillights, and carefully match paint colors. No details are overlooked. Dates with their significant other turn into trips to the RV junkyard (the lucky ones have spouses who see this as an appropriate outing) and hours are spent on the lookout for the next project. No distance is too great to travel to score that next big fix—the rare, the coveted, or the reminder of times long ago. Here are their stories.

SHARI

When you think of restoring trailers, you think of burly men in smelly old garages, not of pretty women with perfect French manicures. Shari is one of the growing number of women who ask for power tools for Christmas and find fulfillment in tearing apart and rebuilding trailers. From Airstreams and a Curtis Wright, on down to her latest project, a Serro Scotty, Shari finds joy in perfection and knowing every nuance about the trailers she rebuilds. Her story started long ago, and like many it is grounded in memories of her youth that have come full circle.

Shari grew up in California near the Airstream factory and remembers driving by the company's billboard. She was fascinated, but her family were tent campers. However, she remembers vividly seeing an Airstream at a campground and her Dad saying, "See that over there? That is one of those Airstreams. If you can have one of those, you are really camping in style!"

Fast forward many years, when she was traveling for the Christmas holiday to see her parents in Arizona, playing a silly road game with Rob, her husband: let's count the Airstreams! Little did she know that game was about to change her life. Talking about it on the way home, Rob agreed that if she could find a trailer, they would get one. Two weeks later, on January 19, while getting ready to go to a cat show (to find her cat a boyfriend), they spotted an Airstream for sale in the classifieds, just blocks from their house.

They stepped inside the trailer for the first time (the first time they had ever been in an Airstream) and thought, "This is a pretty good deal, we can do this!" The excitement built as another car pulled up and people piled out as though it were a clown car. They, too, were there to buy their trailer. Of course, Shari and her husband had first rights, but their minds started racing—where would they find cash on a weekend? They didn't have that kind of money lying around, but they had already decorated the trailer in their mind, and this was their trailer! Luckily, those were the days when you could write a check and you had a few days to arrange your finances. So they wrote a rubber check until they could move money into their account and ran around like crazy making arrangements to pick up their new trailer.

Birdy's front window view peeking into her kitchen with a sweet vintage marshmallow tin perched on her counter.

Birdy, the beautifully restored 1956 Airstream Safari, sits gleaming in the sunlight.

There is nothing like an Airstream sitting in wildflowers. Birdy is at a music festival nestled high in the mountains.

Cocktails in the afternoon are so much better with a trailer view. Birdy serves up ginger martinis.

However, when they called the owner to arrange pickup, they got bad news. "I changed my mind; I am going to let my father-in-law stay in it," he said. Their hearts sank, but two hours later, the owner called back and said they could have the trailer. So off they went before he could change his mind, into the snow, without trailer lights, and without even a place to park it. Maxwell, a 1964 Globetrotter, was on his way home.

They parked it on the street in front of their house in Denver, Colorado, and did what any sane trailerite would do—they called all the neighbors to say "look what we bought!" and invited them over to sit in their new trailer and drink wine. This is where it all began. A price tag of $3,100 for a new Airstream might not sound like much now, but in 1964, when Maxwell was made, the average income was $6,080. A car cost $2,230 and gas to run it was twenty-five cents a gallon. It was a special purchase and people cherished their new silver trailers, the finest on the road. Shari's voice rises in excitement as she talks about the trailers she has refurbished— their blackwater tanks and gopher holes, their windows, plumbing, and the unique attributes of certain layouts. She takes apart heaters and rebuilds them and restores the trailers' original emblems to good as new.

Fully immersed in the lifestyle, Shari became president of the Vintage Airstream Club and spent time helping others on Airstream forums, all the while looking for trailers. Birdy, her current Airstream, was a Craigslist find. The owners were selling it, then not selling it, then selling it again. Finally they had a garage sale and she was able to see the trailer. The conversation with the owners turned to cats, and when they found out her cat's name was Lily Bug, they suddenly perked up. Their grandmother's name was Lily Bird, and the trailer had been her's. So Birdy, a 1956 Safari, found a new home. The remodel that previous owners had done, including sponge painting the birch cabinets, required a full, frame-off restoration. New holding tanks were installed, plumbing and electrical systems were replaced, cabinets were refinished, floors replaced, upholstery redone. Birdy once again gleams like she just rolled off the showroom floor.

Shari also has a Serro Scotty camping trailer under reconstruction. Already new birch walls and a cork floor gleam in the soft light. No challenge is too daunting. After all, when your motto is "if it's worth doing, it's worth overdoing," restorations take on new meaning.

Showing off the distinct row of windows that make the 1956 Safari so special, Birdy sits by a stream with the storms moving in over the mountains behind her.

TONY

From the time he was a curly-haired little boy with an angelic face and sweet smile, Tony liked to tear things apart. He wanted to see how they worked, make them work again, or just make them better. It started with small things like systematically disassembling his sister's doll house, prying open calculators, and tearing apart toys, until his obsession graduated to cars and finally Airstreams.

Some things in life change you and you see nothing but possibilities. You fall in love with an object and want to spend all your time around it. Tony found this kind of love in his Airstream B van. The van started out with the classic Airstream oak cabinets, 1980s mauve and blue upholstery, and granny wallpaper. But the twenty-some-year-old old van had its issues. The ceiling panels were hanging down and mold was found in the ceiling. Wasps had made their home in the furnace exhaust vent, hot water exhaust, and under the air-conditioner cover. The top and plumbing leaked, and the floor had been replaced with unattractive parquet. Tony had never tackled a project like this, but that didn't stop him. He gutted the van, rewiring, insulating, and rebuilding it better than new. White vinyl ceilings were replaced with gray cloth headliner, mauve and blue upholstery became gray leather, wallpaper was transformed into stainless tiles, and dated fixtures were replaced. Oak became bamboo, and party lights were installed. "Farley" has been reborn and people are drawn to the trailer. It isn't unusual to see six or more people

piled in the van, laughing and talking, party lights blinking. Tony has found a soulmate in an old van and plans to spend a good part of his summers in it, fly fishing in the mountains, towing his Jeep, or just being with friends and family. It's a tiny home that offers freedom and security, a place he created out of shambles.

Life isn't always fair, and you can be unexpectedly handed a challenge that is both life-threatening and life-changing. You never know where your strength will come from or what will rise to the top as truly important. When Tony faced such a challenge, his family rose to the top, as well as the desire to wander at will with Farley, to sleep under the stars, to be safe, independent, and free once more..

Farley, the Airstream B Van,
sits on the Arkansas River. Its modest exterior belies
the decidedly modern interior.

Sleek cabinetry and gleaming stainless steel give Farley a distinct look not seen in your typical B Van. A convection microwave, coffee bar, and pop-up counter give the resident chef everything needed to entertain guests.

....

The bamboo floor and leather couch add a touch of luxury. There is a full table for serving guests, a king-size bed above the cab, and a full (however petite) bath.

A gorgeous restoration is finished off with period accessories.

....

Even the diminutive powder room has a unique charm in this gem.

....

Colorful bedding, with the perfectly casual umbrella and hat tossed on the bed, evokes a steamy walk on a hot day.

Warm woods and the soft shine of metal highlight the interior of this exceptionally well-done restoration.

....

No detail is left undone.
Countless hours are poured into a trailer like this,
not only in labor but searching for
the perfect accessories.

New trailers cannot compete
with a beautiful restoration: the depth of the woods,
the curve of the deco-inspired cabinetry.

....

Yacht-inspired interior
is accessorized with chrome hardware and
clever storage solutions.

Curved woods and burgundy leather
cocoon the front dining area of this sweet little trailer.

....

This Jazz Age–inspired renovation has visitors listening
to Bessie Smith while sipping a Gin Rickey.

Art deco splendor evokes the luxury,
glamour, and exuberance of the time.

....

Fedora and jacket casually tossed on the couch
are reminiscent of Gable and Lombard.

....

Chrome deco airplane pays tribute
to the golden age of flight.

Someone has to supply all the parts and pieces for the perfect restoration,
and Vintage Trailer Supply is a favorite.

Chapter Two

Girl camp—Women who travel their own path

Girl Camp has an aura of mystery for the men who aren't allowed. It's a place for women to gather and become girls again, sharing stories and silly games while doing what they love because there is safety in numbers. Traveling far and wide, they accumulate travel tales that you would find hard to believe unless you know them and understand their free spirit. What's a girl to do when she develops vertigo towing her trailer over a Colorado mountain pass? Flag down a couple of truckers and get them to drive it for her! Such are the adventures of the girls at Girl Camp.

A girl has to be practical. Going potty outside is a necessity that sometimes comes with its own hazards.

Girl Camp is filled with the serious and the sublime, and while you never know what will happen next, you can be guaranteed it won't be dull. Girl Campers ponder serious topics, such as surviving the death of a loved one or dating again after divorce, and, of course, the most serious question of all: should you wear underwear to bed? (The answer is no.)

The women surround and protect each other, teach each other to be independent and strong, and give encouragement when a girl needs it most.

Here are their stories.

"Go Pokes" takes on a whole new meaning when a girl hangs her laundry out at Girl Camp.

A real cowgirl and extraordinary entertainer who sings about girls being strong and independent,
Juni Fisher gives a concert perched atop a trailer in a pasture in Buffalo, Wyoming.

A cupcake-sweet vintage trailer dressed in pink and lace is a perfect glamping spot.

....

Tickled Pink is a confection of vintage perfection.

Free as a Bird is perched on a mountaintop in the Colorado mountains in a camp of women.

PAM

"The pursuit of truth and beauty is a sphere of activity in which we are permitted to remain children all our lives."
—Albert Einstein

Someone once told Pam, remember the child in you, the child that was once you. That piece of advice has burned in her all these years. Burned as she raised her family and prepared for a time when she could wander unencumbered, free to discover the girl still living inside.

The little pink Shasta
sits at a roadside stop on a lonely, forgotten highway.

When she discovered it on eBay, the curve of the vintage Shasta called to her seductively, the wings reminding her of freedom. She knew instinctively that this was the one, something she could call "mine" at this stage in her life.

The iconic Route 66. The Mother Road. Chicago to Santa Monica, 2,448 miles of americana. The minute that Sisters on the Fly® posted the meetup event, Pam signed up, even though she was one of the first to do so. She knew she had to accomplish this goal: Chicago to Santa Monica through rain, hail, and tornado warnings.

Historic Route 66 is the road of dreams for vintage trailer enthusiasts.

The allure of the road called to her. The sinuous curve of the winding pavement, the clattering of tires on wooden bridges, the long-forgotten towns along the way. Following the route of those who migrated west to California looking for a better life during the Dust Bowl in the 1930s gives one a sense of history and an appreciation for the hardships they endured. Pam could sense the family vacations taken by car in the 1950s from the rusty signs still swinging in the desert air, motels made to look like teepees at the Wigwam Village, and the Blue Swallow with its refrigerated air beckoning families who piled into station wagons for their annual pilgrimage. Generations traveling together in a tradition long lost. Mom, dad, grandparents, and children all feeling the excitement of the road. Pam wanted the same experience—not to fly over America, but to feel it under her feet, sleep under the stars, and see it with her own eyes. Her goal is simple: to keep living life to the fullest in the little pink Shasta that gave her wings to fly.

Curling up with a great novel is the perfect afternoon pastime. This is the place to reflect, dream, or just relax and escape the world.

Warm birch and a tiny chandelier frost this pink Shasta. No detail is left undone, down to the toile towel draped on the stove.

....

Polka-dot sheers blend with candy-striped curtains in this cozy booth, the perfect place to take your afternoon tea.

Bodacious Ta Ta's sits in dappled sunlight
at a girl camp.

Little Dot has lots of, well, dots, and cute accessories
including a suitcase table.

A big girl camp welcome!
Chandelier, lace, cowboy boots, and flamingos
are the cost of entry.

....

"We were going to change the world today,
but then something sparkly caught our eye."

Welcome to open house at a girl camp. Laundry out?
Check. Cookies? Check. Ironing board and fresh flowers? Check and check.

Nothing else to be said,
other than,
"God Bless Cowgirls!"

....

Quilts, lace, and chenille
make this little Shasta trailer
a perfect retreat.

....

Even Barbie is channeling
her cowgirl!

Much like people, trailers age with character
that can't be replicated.

....

The happy little Fiesta sits on the plains,
camping with friends.

A field of sunflowers spreads sunnily across this cute little trailer
with its idyllic farm scene.

We can smell the fresh tortillas frying in the pan, waiting to be served on the vintage tablecloth.

Like the pillow says, it ain't easy being queen!

Mexican pots and warm red upholstery highlight the décor in this special space.

An old yellow Shasta has winged its way to the Sandhills
to enjoy a peaceful weekend away.

The galley area is complete with a gun-motif towel holder, chalkboard cabinets, and rodeo poster.

·······················

It's a good question:
How much fun can you have before you go to hell?

·······················

It's a western serape theme in this girl's camper, designed as a party spot for all her friends to circle around its round table.

·······················

Girls camp in all sorts of unexpected places. They gather like a string of colorful beads dropped on the prairie grass.

Fearlessly traveling across the nation, girls camp in the most unexpected places.

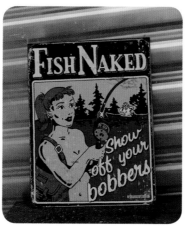

The iconic Wigwam Motel in Holbrook, Arizona, a kitschy and fun place to stop for the night.

....

Every cowgirl needs a little support at camp, so customized lingerie is not uncommon.

....

Girls fish. And they do occasionally show their "bobbers."

Vardo-inspired opulence awaits you
in this well-appointed boudoir.

....

A gypsy-themed trailer at girl camp.
We can see our future in the crystal ball and it
includes more trailers.

Every trip can be a safari, especially when you have a wild trailer like this one.

Beddy Bye sports a robin's-egg-blue stove and vintage accessories.

....

"Reel" women fish and wear pink!

LORI

The Alaska-Canadian Highway in the 1960s, with its many steep grades, switchbacks, dirt surface, and few guardrails, is the background for some of Lori's most treasured memories. She traveled this fabled route as a nine-year-old with her mother and father in a classic canned ham trailer, a Trail-Along. A day of travel over the unpaved roads meant spending the night in a dust-covered trailer. However, her resourceful father found an old oriental carpet to drape over the trailer to keep out some of the dirt. Add to that the caribou horns he procured for the car hood, and you can imagine the odd sight they made on their return trip through the city.

Memories like this last a lifetime, and you never know what will bring them to the surface. For Lori it was an ordinary Saturday and a chance encounter at Barnes and Noble, where a small group of vintage trailer aficionados were gathered for a book signing. One look and the feelings came flooding back. She needed a trailer.

This galley is perfectly appointed with everything you need to pack a picnic lunch for an afternoon of fishing.

A place to relax before heading down the long, lonely road.

After many disappointing missed deals, the Jolly Rancher entered her life. The warm birch paneling, the sweet wooden screen door with a little sliding door, and the authentic soul of the camper were all perfect, but what sealed the deal was the layout. It was identical to the little camper that traveled the long road when she was nine. She was smitten.

For Lori, it is a cross between a doll house she can dress up with Christmas lights and a small silver tree with vintage ornaments, and a time machine. Lori can sit in the familiar camper and go back to a simpler time. She is home, on the road again, with her parents watching from afar, smiling and laughing with her.

The Jolly Rancher is all vintage charm and warmth.

Sunny, warm, and charming.
It just doesn't get better than this.

....

Gathering flowers, weaving wreaths,
and making every space feel like home
—all in a day's work.

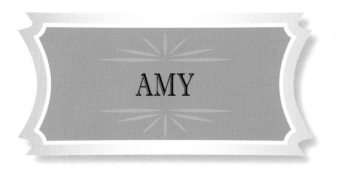

AMY

Sometimes you come across someone who sees life a little differently, but rarely do you run across it packaged in a petite blonde full of unbridled energy. With an affinity for the beauty that surrounds her, Amy prefers to be camping in forests and next to creeks, and like many, her passion for the outdoors started young. Memories of camping in a big green tent in Washington State—Mount Rainier, Mount St. Helens—are so fresh in her mind

she can still smell the damp canvas. Of course, Amy also remembers the rain and cold, shivering in the old tent and wishing she could have one of those cute little campers that always parked near them. One day she ran across a gathering of these campers and her passion was reignited.

Girls need flowers, and ways to display them.

Cowgirl Up was originally a hunting trailer, owned by her nephew's grandfather. It needed structural work, but the price was right, so the 1975 Rancho Del Rey followed her home one day and underwent a decidedly Western makeover. An old trunk holds supplies on the tongue of the trailer and bandana bunting complements the custom paint job. Flowers are a must for any girl camp, and find a place in Cowgirl Up's décor.

You will find Amy and her little piece of the Old West parked along a river, stream, mountain ridge, or in the forest, where she can relive the sights and smells of her cherished childhood.

Cowgirl Up's custom paint—yee-ha!

Sit by the river, strum your guitar, and relax in front of Cowgirl Up.

Hot as a chili pepper, cowgirls know how to party in their vintage trailers.

....

Cowgirl Up sports a leather storage trunk and bandana bunting.

Chapter Three

Aluma fever—Airstreams and the people who crave them

The allure of an Airstream is undeniable. Their shiny skins evoke adventure and romance to celebrities and commoners alike. Airstream enthusiasts gather in groups across the country to talk about their shared passion and to ask each other, "So, how many do you have?" because the answer is seldom just one.

A vintage Airstream is perched on a hill; mother and daughter relax with a bottle of wine.

The iconic Airstream, one of our most recognized pieces of Americana.

Nothing gives Airstreamers more pleasure than showing them off. Purists see them as time capsules and keep them looking just like they did when they rolled off the factory floor. Others want to make them their own. They wallpaper, shine, paint, decorate, and bedazzle. Some owners modify and modernize while others pile on the kitsch. One thing is certain—no two are the same, and you never know what you will find in an Airstream. Here are their stories.

DAN

Little boys dream of being firemen, astronauts, or superheroes. Then real life hits and they become teachers, janitors, and salesmen (has any boy really wanted to become a salesman?). Dan is one of the lucky ones. He spent his life as a fireman, then bought himself a spaceship that reminded him of his childhood and Flash Gordon—a 1959 Airstream Traveler that looked like it could fly.

Old boxes, a little rope, and some lights to make sure you find your way in the dark. Dan has made the perfect accessory for his trailer.

The ability to park in a meadow, fish in the stream, listen to the birds, and watch the wildlife scamper by— an Airstream is perfect for this coveted lifestyle.

He found it behind his workplace, in the backyard of a couple of guys who seemed to have a yard sale every week. They would camp out in the yard and fill it with odd garage sale finds. The trailer had belonged to a former oil driller, the late brother of one of the guys. It was filled with tools, polyester clothing, and Hai Karate that he had left behind.

After fixing the shrunken tiles, soft spots on the floor, and other ailments, Dan filled it with vintage Pendleton blankets, afghans made by his mother, and other mementos of a life well lived. It is chock full of vintage charm, like the copper cover over the heater and the enamel stove. Dan has had several trailers, but this one is a keeper. After all, where would he find another one?

A 1959 Airstream Traveler glows in the mountain sun.
Its old skins have the soft patina only time can achieve.

LOIS

There is always one memory from childhood we hold onto vividly, one that seems like yesterday, that intertwines throughout the rest of your life. Lois has a memory of standing in front of McDonald's with her daddy and seeing an Airstream drive by. She didn't know exactly what it was, only that it was shiny and beautiful and it spoke to her, and she tilted her face up and said, "Daddy, someday I am going to have one of those!" This obsession took forty years to see through.

Every campsite needs fresh flowers.

An Airstream International at Angel Fire, New Mexico.

Lois's find is a 1978 Airstream Tradewind resplendent in its original harvest gold décor, including the couch upholstery, and original tambour doors, mattresses, and box springs. An elderly gentleman reluctantly gave it up, as his daughter was concerned he would fall. It is not unusual to see people lined up on the couch, eating homemade cookies and taking in the old trailer's ambiance. This family trailer was never meant to be fancied up. It is meant to create memories for those lucky enough to be invited in.

For Lois, the joy of finally owning an original Airstream is tempered by the memory of the owner, tears rolling down his weathered face as he watched her drive it away. The story is heartbreaking and heartwarming all at once, since this little trailer has found a new family to love it, be a caretaker, and give it the life on the road it deserves.

This old girl sits in a campground at a rally, surrounded by rose-colored rock that reflects off her time-worn skin.

JOHNNY B. GOODE

Not all decisions in life are deliberate. Some are the result of circumstances, like the loss of a life partner. The Airstream lifestyle was foreign to Johnny, an antique dealer. He thought traveling around in trailers was for old people, not something that someone in the prime of their life would consider. But then he met a woman

Pops of color spell out home for Johnny B. Goode.

Like badges of honor, stickers proudly show where the Airstream has been.

named Shirley and his perspective changed. Suddenly, being cocooned in aluminum felt comforting. The trailer was something he could travel in and use to share his passion for music. Johnny and Shirley travel the country in their little silver home on wheels bringing music to the people who need it most at gatherings and campgrounds across the country. Life is different now, but still something to revel in. No one is a stranger, all are invited in to feel the music of his life and join him in the dance.

FRED

This 1953 Flying Cloud was the first one made at the Ohio Airstream factory.

When you hear the word historian, you think of someone in a dim room poring over musty old books and papers. But if you follow the Airstream lifestyle, you think of Fred, a delightful man with twinkling eyes, a penchant for disco music, and an encyclopedic knowledge of Airstreams. Mention of the smallest detail is enough to send him off researching every nuance of the subject. His enthusiasm is infectious.

An attorney by trade, an author by choice, Fred has been able to apply his professional skills to something he really cares about: iconic American brands. His long-time interest in camper trucks and trailers developed into a focus on teardrop trailers. After researching them for a year, he decided he was too old to crawl into small spaces and cook outside in the rain. His interest then turned to Airstream trailers. He applied for membership in the Wally Byam Airstream Club (WBCCI), but without a trailer he was denied access to the exclusive group. (Wally Byam founded Airstream.) So he sought out his first Airstream.

He found it in a chance encounter during a trip to his favorite truck junkyard. Detouring on a back road, he came upon a man selling old lawn mowers, but in the backyard was an Airstream trailer—an eighteen-foot 1953 Clipper, one of the last ones made. It was just a shell, but it gained him entrance into the club. He towed the empty shell to his first vintage rally in Wichita Falls,

Its gleaming skin reflects the surrounding flora.

Ruby, a 1948 Wee Wind, peeks out from behind a fence where she is protected.

Texas, where the wheels of his destiny were set in motion. Someone suggested that Fred become the vintage Airstream historian, an official-sounding title that gained him access to the Airstream factory archives, which was his goal all along.

He now possesses a more complete archive of technical information than the Airstream factory itself, including materials from the estate of Dale Schwamborn (Wally Byam's cousin once removed).

Fred knows trailers made before 1968. After that, the body style changed, and he lost interest. Early Airstreams were designed with input from people who actually used them, which gives the old trailers a much different feel than the later ones. Executives hit the road a couple times a year to meet with customers, who had a feel for the mechanics.

Acrylic glass curves seductively across the front of the Liner. The gold anodized tops of the rivets are just visible in the never-polished, unspoiled skin.

Oh, the places she's been.

The original center taillight still graces the old trailer; temporary lights can be added for transport safety.

Fabricated hinges highlight a postwar manufacturing technique.

The logo position on this Airstream is unusual, as logos were typically put on the front or back, not on the sides. This side placement was seen most often on Wally Byam's trailers (often at the top of an interior door) or on demos for McFaul Brothers, dealers in Los Angeles.

The original propane tank sits proudly among the wildflowers. The T-handle screw jack is another rare original feature.

Serial number 3003, the third Wee Wind made.
The highest serial number documented is 3054, indicating at least
fifty-four were made. Less than ten are known to survive.
Costing $1,495 in 1948, it was pricey for a time when
minimum wage was forty cents an hour.

These round-end trailers were called "liners," and Ruby is one of less than ten known to exist. Only about half of those are known to be in original condition, with Ruby identified as the most original. Serial number 3003 means she was the third one made. Fred lovingly refers to her as a "sweet old gal" as he describes her original yellow paint (this was pre-zolatone and came in tender green or yellow), acrylic windows, dried-out floor tiles, one-brake light, glass bee-hive lenses, radio antenna, and door-in-door. She has a hook under her light to hang a Coleman gas lantern on and a window that spans partially into the closet. But the most amazing feature is the upholstery. Protected all these years by slipcovers, even the ribbon from the upholsterer sits untouched under a button. Every nuance is perfect in its minimalism.

Fred likes to revel in the past. His passion isn't about collecting objects, it's about collecting history and preserving a bygone era.

A 1953 Flying Cloud is his current go-to trailer; it replaced his 1964 Globetrotter because the layout suited his lifestyle better. The rear double bed, front dinette, and shower was a configuration he first saw at a homecoming at Jackson Center (every year, owners are invited to bring their Airstreams "home" to the factory).

As much technical knowledge as Fred has, you can detect a change in his posture and tone when he speaks about Ruby, a 1948 Airstream Wee Wind. Fred is her second caretaker. The original owners, Harry and Ruby Mann, purchased her in 1948 in Los Angeles, then took her home to Las Vegas. The little trailer spent most of her life near the old downtown, snuggled under the covered porch of their cinder block ranch house.

Harry ran a gun shop at the New Frontier Hotel and Casino (the second resort to open on the Vegas strip, it operated continuously from October 30, 1942, to July 16, 2007). He was known as the "sportsman to the stars" and took celebrities on hunting and fishing excursions in the trailer. If only it could talk. Sadly, Harry passed away in 1960, and the trailer continued its life under the covered porch until Ruby passed away as well.

Buttercream walls glow against the original cabinetry's
rounded corners. The window goes partly into the closet for light,
yet another simple design feature that makes sense
in a trailer meant to be used.

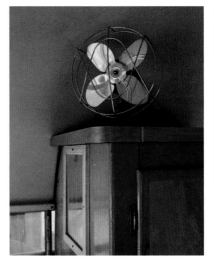

Ruby's unvented butane
heater was a sufficient
heat source, but is certainly
not up to today's codes.

The galley is snug against the trailer's lounge area. At 16 feet, every inch is well used.
An original upholsterery tag from I. Gruda Upholstery in Culver City, California, graces this pristine example
of postwar modern industrial design. The kitchen features a three-burner gas stovetop and a sink that hooks
to the campground's cold water source.

I like big butts, and I cannot lie ... Airstream butts, that is.
All lined up in Alma, Colorado.

The New Mexico desert
is softly reflected in the shiny
aluminum
of this old beauty.

....

An Airstream International
waits for afternoon storm clouds
to roll in over the mountains.

Dents record Airstreams' past lives.
Ghosts of owners past lurk on many an
old Airstream, like 20844.

....

Even our littlest friend, the hummingbird,
is attracted to the shiny silver skin.

A camp crane flies the American flag.

....

A vintage Airstream parked along a bubbling river peeks out
from behind an old shed in the Colorado mountains.

Buttercup sits under storm clouds, waiting for the rain to cool her aluminum skin.

New Year's Day in the Rockies.
Nothing stops a gathering of friends, not even a little weather.

Early morning in Lake Tahoe.

An Airstream wears a
cap of snow.

....

Trade Wind travel stickers
old and new. If only this trailer
could talk.

FRANK

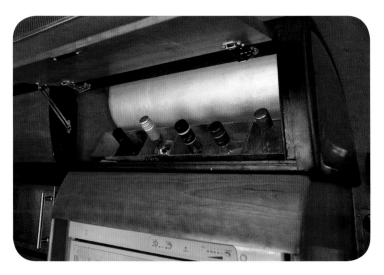

Awkward space above the refrigerator becomes a lighted bar.

Frank is an artist who sees no limitations. At first you are horrified; who would do this to an Airstream when there are purists who spend hours polishing out every scratch to achieve that mirror shine. But then you find yourself inexplicably drawn in. Suddenly, it seems like a good idea to etch a twenty-foot shark and an octopus on the side of the trailer, that mermaids belong on bathroom doors, and that shark eyes should glow. The Airstream becomes an opus, an opportunity to make another sculpture come to life regardless of medium.

Frank came to own the Sharkstream out of necessity. A life-long backpacker, his body started to protest sleeping on the hard ground, and after losing two tents in the wind while pursuing his other hobby, sailing, the idea of a trailer just made sense. He bought it with a friend from college, Don, who had always wanted an Airstream, so their path was set. It would be an Airstream they shared, renovated, and took on adventures across the country. The shark part came later.

After renovating the interior, Frank's thoughts turned to the outside. As a yachter, he knew it would have a nautical theme and be inspired by his family's boat, *The Jolly Codgers*. Frank invited family members to submit ideas for the exterior. The final design was a giant octopus ensnaring a shark on the starboard side, with another shark taking a substantial bite out of the same octopus on the port side.

The design was etched into the aluminum with wire wheels, brushes, and Scotch Brite pads. The old trailer's imperfections became part of the composition, such as the foot-and-a-half-long gash that is part of a fish; taxidermy shark eyes that glow in the dark were added for extra drama. Like many art installations, the Sharkstream is continually refined as the artists work their magic.

Is tattooing an Airstream for everyone? Probably not. But where will you ever see another one?

The Sharkstream depicts
underwater drama.

....

A shark and octopus tangle
on the Airstream. When the lights go on,
the shark's eye glows red.

Chapter Four
Vintage style—Trailer décor

Décor is subjective. Should it be true to the trailer and period correct? Or maybe you should go with a theme? And then there are the aficionados of pure kitsch who dress these trailers to the hilt like fancy French poodles on parade. There is no limit to the imagination or the styles with which people decorate their trailers.

Much like a playhouse from childhood, outfitting a vintage trailer represents an opportunity to let our inner child run wild. To add and subtract as whim strikes us and step into our fantasy world, even if it's only for a short time. Every garage sale, junk store, and auction is ripe with decorating possibilities. Old ironing boards become bars, chandeliers are made from every conceivable material, and Melmac dishes are carefully matched to curtains.

Wedding photos and gas lanterns makes perfect sense at this camp.

No vintage trailer is complete without the requisite pink flamingo.

Leopard wallpaper? Sure, why not? Anything that reminds you of Granny is immediately invited in, as are things from your childhood. Not all is kitsch, however. Sometimes the most unexpected things are found.

What if you dream of time travel? Not a problem, you can blur the lines between fact and fiction. Whatever strikes your fancy is what lands in a vintage trailer. Here are the stories.

Sunny yellow and warm birch tones cheer the interior.
The tea-dyed bunting curtain lends vintage flair.

Turquoise, yellow, and frosted with lace, a girl's doll house dream come true.

Some trailers are just plain cute, like this one with its vintage icebox and homey décor.

....

A peek though the screen door reveals a loving restoration.

A hammered copper refrigerator and sheepskin lend glamour to this bunkhouse.

Sticks serve as curtain rods under an old barn lantern.

....

Cowhide coexists with leather and lace.

Gingham and Coke make any trailer sweeter.

It's the Real Thing, a camper theme loved by many.

HARRY

Airstream Clipper meets steampunk accessories.

Steampunk. According to Urban Dictionary, steampunk is a subgenre of speculative fiction, usually in an anachronistic Victorian or quasi-Victorian setting. It could be described by the slogan, "What the past would look like if the future had happened sooner."

Harry first heard the term steampunk at a car show when looking at a car that intrigued him. It was a paradigm shift for him and the Airstream Clipper he had at home waiting for a remodel. He had envisioned it as a 1940s cabin, but that idea started to transform.

He haunted garage sales, estate sales, and junk shops searching for mundane objects that could evolve with his vision. Two years of shopping and imagining brought out his dormant artist, and he started piecing the collected parts together. Would that copper Jell-O mold pair with the old glass he found last month? What about those old gears and bottles? He would sit in his empty trailer with a bottle of wine and visualize his creation, moving away from his original vision of "Yosemite Sam" to the current scheme: his own time machine.

Think Wild, Wild, West, where stained glass meets copper gadgetry. Persian carpets cover the floor, while a presider's chair serves as a place to rest while dialing in your ultimate destination. Dials and apparatuses commingle with the more practical elements like ion collectors. The soul of Jules Verne is reborn, or at least channeled, through Harry: avant-garde in 3-D.

A fully stocked apothecary stands by as you hurtle through space and time.

Strap yourself into the oak chair, slip your feet into the chrome slippers, and see where your imagination takes you. Forward or backward, the only limit is your mind.

Close inspection is advised when decamping to parts unknown.

The little Airstream Clipper is a magnet for karma. Harry found an old chair and was searching for a table to pair it with. Up in the rafters of his barn for the past nine years was his wife's grandmother's table, rough and rickety. Harry suddenly thought of it as he came across another table with a great base but unusable top. He brought it down from the rafters and flipped it over. Stenciled into the wood was the word "Clipper." Synchronicity. Grandma's table was meant to be brought back to life to live in the time machine.

His friends are fascinated. They bring gifts of homage to the trailer. Old cast iron water pumps; what could he do with that? Photos that have spiritual meaning to both giver and receiver find their way into the trailer, such as Chief Little Raven (also known as Hosa), which will bring peace to the travelers who enter.

Harry's time machine actually works. It takes you on a flight of fancy like no other artist has been able to do. Time travel is possible

Time travel can be
exhausting; every traveler needs
a place to rest his head.

· ·

There's always time for a
cup of tea.

Even time travel demands the basics,
like light to find your way.

· ·

Will one of these gadgets find the
elusive wormhole?

Part Wild, Wild West, part unbridled imagination,
the time machine has many nuances.

....

Which key will you turn to land in the perfect time period?
Or, could it be you're already there?

Only the wizard behind this creation knows what every gauge, lever, and key controls.

A step-saver kitchen: everything
a homemaker needs.

....

Warm birch walls are the perfect backdrop
to Barkcloth drapes.

The Cardinal Deluxe maintains its original charm.

The Cardinal Deluxe was built in El Monte,
California, and sold for around $1,000—a fraction
of what you would pay for one in
good condition today.

This is how we roll, with a cozy spot to enjoy a View Master on a rainy afternoon.

· ·

Neat as a pin: the Cardinal has a sunny yellow stove and period-perfect accessories.

Orange appliances and sink are reminiscent of a summer Creamsicle.

....

Tin toys are a favorite decorator item in vintage trailers, but this VW bus is unusual.

MARY

Not all who seek fulfillment travel. Sometimes satisfaction comes in the form of a little vintage trailer that never leaves the yard. Yard art that serves as the Secret Garden of literary fame. A place to relax and reflect, or a camping experience for grandchildren, providing memories that will last a lifetime.

A covered porch is the perfect place to keep an eye on your yard-trailer.

Petite patio.

Fairy gardens grace a porch where you can relax in vintage metal chairs, the sounds of mooing cattle mixed with the laughter of children as they plan their next big adventure in the backyard hideaway. The trailer is a life-size playhouse ripe with possibilities. Ghost stories replace video games, lanterns replace electric lamps, and big feather comforters replace mechanical heat. Big old farm dogs become your playmates while barn cats lurk in the tall grass, trying to catch mice and butterflies.

Life on a ranch continually evolves. You spend your life there, but your children are replaced with grandchildren, and the love of your life moves on to a better place. But one thing never changes: the peace and solitude of the trailer.

The garden Cardinal surrounded by flights of fancy and cattle. You don't have to leave home to dream in this special spot.

....

Hosting campouts and slumber parties doesn't require long trips; the backyard is just fine.

Meet Lil' Chick. Chirp!
This 1964 Thunderbolt is a vision of fluffy
yellow perfection.

....

Lil' Chick has a sweet little kitchen
with everything you need, including the
requisite chandelier.

An iron bed in a trailer?
Of course you can!

....

Lil' Chick speaks.
Lil' Chick from the back.

Not all is kitsch. Vintage Harris Strong
tiles adorn this little home.

....

Through the looking glass:
the door mirror is a window in time,
a throwback to a simpler life.

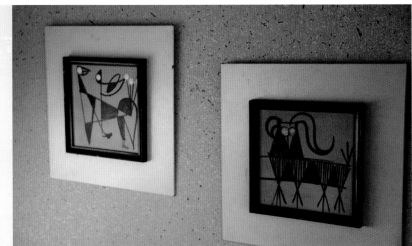

The honey-colored wood and green vinyl are pitch perfect.

Warm woods and old porcelains lend a cabin feel.

Wrap-around windows make the Holiday House one of the most coveted vintage trailers.

A road trip to the '70s.

A renovation features gleaming stainless counters and honey-kissed wood. Art deco barware awaits afternoon cocktails.

....

The perfect farmhouse kitchen,
just add the chicken for Sunday dinner.

Delightfully authentic, right down to the wire dish drainer and wall-mount can opener.

Original starburst linoleum is just one of the details that make this trailer distinct.

....

Car-style seats in robin's-egg-blue perk up this charming caravan.

Vintage metal flamingos wade through
the grass at a trailer show.

....

Old barn wood adds charm
that's missing from newer models.

A 1965 Arrow trailer sports special touches
such as a Sitting Bull sign and canvas water bag.

....

Western themes abound in vintage trailers,
and this 1965 Arrow even has arrow curtain rods.

Vintage tins and coffee grinder
add ambiance.

....

Dinner is served on the
Fire King jadeite dinnerware.

A lounge area with simplicity and soul.

Pretty in pink,
with the pièce de résistance—polka dots!
A 1959 Streamline Prince,
all original and pristine.

....

Original pink walls and a frise couch
are reminiscent of grandma's parlor,
complete with doilies.

Frisé and lace—this house
on wheels is the real deal.

....

Ruffled lampshades and porcelain clocks
are just a few of the details inside
this vintage jewel.

Beautiful old wood surrounds
the original white enamel Frigidaire. Molded Jell-O,
fried chicken, and custard pie are sure
to be found inside.

....

The bed beckons.

Beaching it.
Oh, the places you'll go.

....

Flamingos dance across the
trailer in 3-D.

A pink confection,
sweeter than a bakery cupcake.

....

Pink lace curtains enclose this boudoir
filled with ballerinas and rag dolls.

A touch of red is always the perfect accessory, especially this coveted Dixie stove.

There is no better place to cuddle up
after a long day on the water. The top bunk even lets
guests stay over.

....

Surf's up!
This cute rendition of a surf shack
is full of original features.
Even Shubie could call it home.

A 1958 Shasta, easily identifiable by the classic birch magazine rack with the prominent "S" script.

The 1940s live on in this kitchen, with its Modern Maid range.

....

Aluminum measuring utensils and a sought-after spice rack add period touches.

Sometimes you find a trailer where everything just works.

You can't go wrong with a touch of leopard, especially when the heels have tikis carved on them.

....

Turquoise and burlap give this little Nomad a Polynesian flair.

Nothing says vintage like the color red.

....

Raffiaware and custom Barkcloth curtains
set the tone in this travel cabin.

Chapter Five

Tin can fever—The collectors

Collectors dream of the next big find lurking in alleys, around small towns, forgotten in fields, and on the Internet. One trailer is never enough, or two, or really, what's one more? You can never have enough, because they are all different and spark something new with their soul.

No matter the condition, collectors visualize what it will become with just a "little work." Like the gentleman whose neighbor was housing chickens in vintage trailers and offered him one of the better specimens if he could find a replacement coop in twenty-four hours. Did he manage it? Of course he did. Like all good collectors, he has a network of like-minded folks who know where all types of trailers are located at any time. Here are their stories.

One of Jim's trailers, the 1966 Airstream Tradewind is parked at Sweetwater River Ranch next to the Arkansas River.

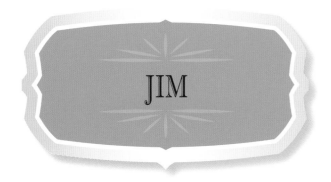

JIM

A farmer at heart, Jim is content only when working with his hands and shaping something new or restoring the past. He found his calling when he went to his first vintage trailer rally and saw the gleaming Airstreams lined up in rows. He told his wife, "This is going to get expensive," and it did as he began bringing old trailers home. He appreciates each of them for what they are and doesn't try to change them. That's not to say he doesn't make

Bathtub, shower, and sink are strategically placed.

A 1966 Airstream kitchen with Sunbeam mixer and Kromex canisters.

small improvements, like lovingly removing the screws, cleaning the skin, and replacing them with new stainless steel screws. But a microwave, flat-screen television, or modern air conditioner will never sit in his old trailers. It just wouldn't seem right. Lovingly named, each specimen has a special meaning to him and brings something new that ignites his imagination.

The 1966 Airstream Tradewind, Stella, has an art deco feel and was discovered at a horse trailer sales lot. Her previous owner had her in for repairs, and when so many people stopped and asked if she was for sale, he decided it was time to find her a new home. Jim scored the sale and immediately began removing the beds, curtains, and sofa so they could be restored. He used gallons of Krud Kutter to clean every inch of the old trailer. Period accessories hunted from far and wide complete the ambiance.

Interior of the lovingly restored 1966 Airstream Tradewind, Stella.

Original bunks float above the twin beds—
a perfect spot for children or extra storage at night.

....

Simple canvas bunks, a rare find,
are stretched over an aluminum frame suspended
by cables. The bunks slide into metal holders under
the cabinets for traveling.

Tillie, the pristine 1970 Serro Scotty, has a coveted jalousie door.

His 1970 Serro Scotty gaucho, Tillie, is the holy grail. She is an original, right down to her curtains. Sitting in an airplane hangar for thirty years, she escaped the plight of most of these inexpensive campers—water damage. A good cleaning, some minor repairs, new screws, and she was back on the road again.

With its speckle paint, curtains, and lighting, the Serro Scotty
is as original as it gets!

Serro Scotty gaucho.
Original mirror and pristine walls, unmarred by water since this little gem lived inside most of its life.

....

Front view of Jim's Serro Scotty,
sitting behind a fence on the river, camping for
the weekend.

The 1948 Bethany Crusader exterior. Only five were made each year for three years (1948–50) before being discontinued due to production costs. However, the company continued to produce a pop-up camper.

．．．．．．．．．．．．．．．．．．．．．．．．．

A 1948 Bethany Crusader, one of two known to exist, waiting for restoration. As often happens, water leaked around the vent and under windows, causing the most dreaded damage of all—mold.

．．．．．．．．．．．．．．．．．．．．．．．．．

A child's pitcher was found in the Bethany Crusader's kitchen cabinet, along with other forgotten treasures.

Lucille, the rare 1948 Bethany Crusader, was built by missionaries in Minneapolis and is one of two known to survive of the approximately fifteen made. Lucille has her original refrigerator, stove, kerosene heater, and tiny toilet. Where would you put a tiny toilet? Not in a closet, but by the back gaucho covered by an ottoman. It makes for interesting entertaining, for sure.

Filmore, a 1971 Winnebago Renegade with the iconic "eyebrows," turns heads wherever he travels.

A 1971 Winnebago Renegade named Filmore is the only motor home in his collection. The shortest Winnebago of its era, the Renegade was made for only one year under that name. Filmore was loved by his previous family and maintained his period 1970s glory, including harvest gold appliances, a padded dashboard, and wood paneling. Filmore now has period furnishings and takes his new family on short excursions, since getting behind the wheel is like driving a shoebox down the road. Filmore's gas mileage isn't great, but this charming Winnebago attracts attention wherever he goes. He can't sit at a gas station or travel down a road towing his 1960 Croft trailer (he needs accessories!) without someone giving him the thumbs up or asking, "Where did you get the cool 'Bago?"

Interior of Filmore, a rare survivor.

....

Filmore sports a Gemco milk glass
condiment set.

Corning Ware and Kromex sit neatly on the stove, just like they would have in 1971.

....

Harvest gold gets on its glow in the late-afternoon sun.

The homemade aluminum teardrop is finally being finished
after more than fifty years.

....

The interior's aluminum cabinets will be preserved.
It's a mystery as to why the trailer was never finished, but the restoration
will give it the respect it deserves.

Rooney, a 1940s teardrop, is homemade entirely of quarter-inch
aluminum, possibly by an airplane mechanic. It appears to have never
been finished and is undergoing restoration, with a concentrated search
for the smallest period details, such as glass lenses for its lights.

....

Ranger Camp trailers were manufactured from 1954 to 1956 in Anaheim, California. They were considered the first modern pop-up camper with only 200 produced.

Sofia, the only pop-up in the assortment, is a 1956 Ranger. Fiberglass with a zolatone interior and birch cabinets, she is a rare survivor of the original 200 production models. Every effort is being made to return her to her original glory, but she doesn't have far to go. The little trailer still has her original curved birch cabinets, Marmoleum flooring, upholstery, icebox, enamel sink, and an oven-range. A lot of cleaning, new paint, and minor repairs, and this mid-century marvel will once again be streaking down the highway, chasing her next big adventure.

Birch cabinets and an original enamel sink, icebox, and stove grace the galley.

A decal survives. A new coat of paint, some cleaning and repairs, and Sofia will be on the road again.

....

This rare survivor still has her original Marmoleum floor.

....

Curved birch cabinets hang above the original upholstery on the beds; the canvas is also original.

The 1955 Airstream Flying Cloud's walls are in fabulous condition, as are the twin-size mattresses and Martha Washington stove. When restored, this will be a gem.

....

The thirteen-panel whale tale with jalousie windows has a soft, even patina on its aluminum skin, so it will not be polished.

Doobie, a thirteen-panel, whale tail 1955 Airstream Flying Cloud, won't need much more than a good cleaning and a few repairs to glow again. Discovered in Wyoming, it sports such original features as a trundle bed under the couch and original twin bed mattresses in the rear. The toilet might horrify a modern-minded camper, but it delights Jim. You can see the ground through the potty hole, where you would have dug a gopher hole for your blackwater or put a bucket under the trailer to hold waste. This was the Cadillac of trailers in its time, but there is no fancy, chemical-filled holding system.

Jim's search never ends, and every trailer calls to him. Someday he might take to the road in one of his creations. Or maybe he will just park and live in them. One thing is certain, when people ask, "Do you ever sell your trailers?" Jim says, "Not yet." He loves them as only a collector could.

A toy collection showcases all kinds of trailers with period-correct cars.

This is how you build your own trailer park—in miniature. Models will do.

···

The Pismo Beach Vintage Trailer Rally featured an impressive display of toys. Think of the time spent searching for a collection of this size.

LUKE

A Wally Bee sits protected in dappled sunlight. Luke is bringing the fiberglass Airstream back to life.

Collector, tinker, and purveyor of miscellany, Luke has just one mission in life: not to be tied to a desk but free to play with his many projects. The business he has established to help others with their projects gives him the freedom to tinker with his own. In addition to fire trucks and popcorn poppers, Luke has a passion for Airstream trailers. At first it looks innocent enough. When you ask how many he has, the answer is three and a half, but that number quickly grows to five and a half (currently, that is).

How does one have half a trailer? You own half, and the half trailer he owns isn't just any Airstream, it's the 1968 Barstream. The Barstream started as a trailer that a tree fell on. What do you do with such a project? You turn it into a mobile bar with the most unusual décor and a stripper pole, of course! The people who love the little trailer donate all kinds of outrageous accessories. Tinsel flamingos, high heels, dinosaurs, photographs, and strings of lights have all made it to the bar. And automatic Jiffy-Pop poppers add the snack element to the ice-cold beer on tap. The trailer's official name is Rist Canyon Bar & Grill and Community Center.

The Wally Bee, a 1956 prototype fiberglass Airstream, is by far the rarest in Luke's collection. An *Airstream Life* article published in 2007 mentioned that no one knew the whereabouts of what was believed to be the sole surviving Wally Bee (discovered by Bud Cooper in 2001). Calling on his extensive Airstream network, Luke found the Wally Bee in 2008. He and a friend drove to McAllen, Texas, and trailered what was left of it home to be restored. The trailer's historical significance cannot be overstated, as it is possibly one of a kind. There are rumors of another fiberglass trailer, but none has been found. The Wally Bee made a trip to Central America in 1962, but time and weather took its toll and it was a mere shell of its former self. The Wally Bee is now being rebuilt to its former glory. The way he sees it, if you are going to invest time in something, it might as well have historical value.

The Barstream sits on a frosty morning at its annual pilgrimage to the quaint gathering of friends on New Year's Eve, high in the Rocky Mountains.

Winter, summer, fall, spring, trailer camping knows no limitations.
Luke's Avion truck camper pulls the Barstream.

Luke has two Avion truck campers. (Why two you ask? Why wouldn't one need a twin?) The riveted aircraft construction used in other popular trailers like the Airstream, Spartan, and Silver Stream was the basis of this Michigan-produced trailer. A study in efficiency, the truck campers were designed by hunting enthusiasts to include all the comforts of home, including a tiny loo.

A 1965 Airstream Caravel Rivet was Luke's first trailer. Luke's dream of owning an Airstream was handed down by his father. Growing up on a dairy farm, owning one wasn't practical since vacations were few and far between, but that didn't stop his father from attending the WBCCI annual rally at Wisconsin Dells in 1959. The thought of seeing the trailers he saw in the TV show

Cape Town to Cairo, narrated by Vincent Price, was something to look forward to. Unfortunately Luke's parents never did get their Airstream, but Luke did. When this trailer came up for sale and he said he would think about it, his better half wisely asked, "How much longer are you going to think?" So Rivet entered his life.

The woman who sold Rivet was proud of the fact she had painted it yellow, just like the one Neiman Marcus was offering! Of course, period zolatone paint was one of the first things to go back onto Rivet, but the rest of the decorating was left up to his life partner, Donna, who expertly chose upholstery and accessories to welcome friends to the lake.

Also in the collection are a 1960 Airstream Safari—an eBay score—and an old Airstream used for storage. Others tend to drift in and out, and he never rules out the possibility another one will join his collection permanently. In the meantime, his time is occupied helping other people refurbish their trailers. Growing up on that dairy farm, Luke knew what hard work was, and that to succeed you had to work for it. And he does, but he never works a day in his life because he is doing what he loves.

Rivet, a beautifully restored 1965 Airstream, welcomes you to the lake, or to paradise.

....

The Airstream Caravel
gets ready for its next adventure.

Rivet in his natural habitat, next to a mountain river.

A toaster-camper, proving once again that imagination knows no bounds.

. . . .

Trailers waiting for Luke's magical repair work. Over half make the pilgrimage from out of state, mostly by word of mouth.

Chapter Six
Trailer Palooza — The Gatherings

They meet with friends old and new, laughing and trying new things like toasting marshmallows and filling them with Kahlua, perfecting the technique to prevent the dreaded drip of sweet liquor down your arm. They listen to a live band until the early morning hours, keeping warm with whiskey and homemade strawberry wine. They play silly games for worthless prizes they wouldn't give up for gold, and wish upon shooting stars while huddled around a campfire. All across the country, vintage trailer lovers get together to plot out a year of adventures. They fill fields, town squares, national forests, trailer parks, and beaches.

The Pismo Beach Vintage Trailer Rally is an annual pilgrimage for over 300 vintage trailers.

Welcome to "The Festival in the Clouds."

They plan vacations and weekend getaways all around one precious asset: their trailer.

Some are huge annual gatherings where the price of admission is vintage: your trailer must be at least twenty-five years old. Others are all about the brand. Like secret sororities, each has its own nuances, rituals, and charm. They go for the love of the trailer, but return for the love of the people. Here are their stories.

MIKE

Mike doesn't crave the newest and shiniest; he craves the soul he finds in things well used. He drives a '41 Dodge truck and grew up camping. He decided to buy an old bus and convert it into a camper so that he could head out with friends at a moment's notice. Did his wife think he had lost his mind when he saw an

Peace-out in the magic bus.

old school bus on eBay (converted to a trailer by a man in Kentucky), bought it sight unseen, and flew to Iowa to drive it across the country? Probably. But the idea of sleeping in a tent just wasn't appealing anymore. Then he bought a '98 Bluebird on eBay for parts, flew to Illinois on Christmas Day, and drove it home, too.

Mike's friends have dubbed the camper the Magic Bus for the trips it takes and the friends it makes along the way, like the music festival in Alma, Colorado, where the parked bus quickly filled with friends old and new. Will he eventually trade it in for a newer model? Never. He wants to keep it forever, because his love for the old bus is what makes him who he is.

Converted into an RV, the old bus exudes vintage cool.

Inside are all the creature comforts of home.

························

The GMC bus sits at a music festival and hosts leagues of friends old and new.

STEVE

Not all who come to trailer meetups are there to see and be seen. Some, like Steve, just like the chance to connect with people on a different level, smoke a cigar, and have fun. A California native who married his high school sweetheart, his horticultural career has taken him across the US and abroad, and supports his passion for trailers.

He finds pleasure in both trailers and old cars with a past, like the pickup he purchased that was once owned by actor Steven Seagal. He didn't expect the old truck to come with a story. It was just a little bonus he discovered on the pink slip, but his eyes twinkle as he fondly remembers the unexpected connection to fame. He purchased the truck to pull his '54 Tourette teardrop, since it was a '54, too. It was a natural fit, and another piece of history added to his collection.

Steve also has a 1964 Shasta that is perfect in every detail. Not perfect in the way a restorer would expect, but perfect because it takes him anywhere he wants to go—to the beach, mountains, old trails, and hidden spots along the way. It comes with a storied past, like the bear prints and scratches along the side, and an awning made of old parachutes. It is the perfect travel companion for him and his wife, with Moses the dog riding shotgun.

Homemade wings can fly you anywhere: beach, mountains, prairie, forest, and then home again.

Palm trees wave in the beach breeze as the 1964 Shasta
waits for the family to return.

Picnic baskets all in a row make delightful storage
in a well-thought-out interior.

....

Nothing tastes better than a cup of joe
among friends.

Nothing is quite as fun as a gathering of vintage trailers and their eclectic owners.

....

The Rockin' Wally-B Ranch! This vintage Airstream rally is held every other year, here in Gunnison, Colorado.

Vintage trailer rentals are becoming more popular and are a great way to experience the charm of days gone by.

....

Girls gathered on the Arkansas River enjoy a few days of fly fishing during the caddis hatch.

One cool tow vehicle at Pismo Beach Vintage Trailer Rally.

....

Another fine vintage Chevrolet tow vehicle.

Gorgeous cabinetry in the
fabricated teardrop with fins.

....

The matching cherry-red trio is
hard to beat.

Teardrops don't get much better than this fine example. A barn find, it has survived in mint condition.

....

This aluminum teardrop trailer has a tent that attaches to add living space. It is towed by a pristine Chevy pickup with vintage air-conditioning attached to the window.

A beautiful Ford sits in front of a Jewel trailer at the Pismo Beach Vintage Trailer show.

Two-toned perfection.

A matching red Shasta and
Bel-Air station wagon.

....

Ready for the beach,
this little red Shasta is
Frankie-and-Annette ready.

Little more than a bed on wheels, this tiny teardrop is perfect in its simplicity.

....

Airstreams come in all sizes, including this door-in-door model. Small trailers are coveted due to their ease of towing.

No gathering is complete without a dog.

A 1957 Hanson Custom Coach, the epitome of vintage tin.

Zimair dining area with the soft glow
of mahogany on the walls.

....

Built to emulate an aircraft, Zimair's slogan was
"sky comfort on wheels."

....

A 1957 Airstream Bubble complete
with outside living space.

....

Not all trailers are glamped, or showpieces.
This trailer is hosting a family weekend
of tubing on the river.

The pinnacle of elegance, the Airfloat's golden shell glistens in the California sun.
Airfloat built some of the finest trailer coaches in the nation; they sported distinctive porthole windows.

A peek inside the Bowlus, past the galley and all the way back to the boudoir.

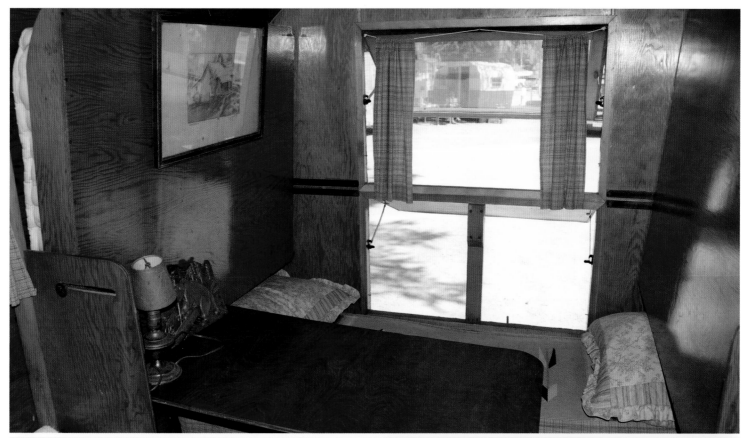

The interior of the elusive Covered Wagon. Constructed of wood with a canvas top, it was considered the first travel trailer.

....

Covered Wagon kitchen with a porcelain sink and wood made by the era's cabinetmakers.

The old man of the vintage trailer show,
the Bowlus Road Chief has a unique bullet shape
and front entry.

. . . .

Its galley gleams with
a patina no modern trailer can match.

. . . .

The blue 1959 Corvette is a cute little tow with jalousie windows.

....

The diminutive 1965 Dethleffs is just one of the unusual trailers you can find at the bigger shows. This is known as the first German caravan and was a study in practicality.

Salmon and cream are a hard combo to beat for a 1950s look.

....

Vintage tow vehicles are a staple at trailer shows. Some are fancy, some utilitarian, but all are there to complement the trailers.

A classic Chevrolet station wagon is painted to match the 1959 Winnebago in the background.

Gongora makes trailer bodies look good!

....

A nice old Cadillac complete with its water bag at Pismo Beach.

An Oasis at the renowned Pismo Beach Vintage Trailer Rally
beckons with the 1937 Pierce-Arrow Travelodge in the background.

No gathering is complete without a smattering of these diminutive teardrop trailers, a study in efficiency.

Vintage buses are also welcome.

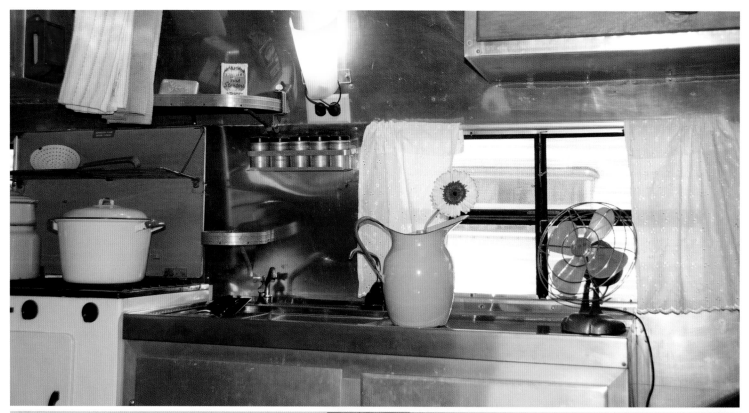

Polished aluminum makes this trailer interior glow.

....

The semi-circular banquette is the perfect place to gather with friends and family for a casual supper, or perhaps a rousing board game.

The rounded ceiling makes
a perfect sleeping spot.

....

One advantage of going
to big trailer rallies is the pure pleasure
of running across an example that
retains its soul.

Everything you need for a hot cup of tea.

....

El fresco dining in style. You can almost hear
the trout frying in the pan.

The velvet bench seating and table display souvenirs like the vintage Grand Canyon pillow and a map to plot your next big adventure.

. . . .

Bunk beds are the perfect place for children.

Chapter Seven
Happily ever after—Life with a trailer view

Enchanted Trails hosts many beautiful old trailers permanently,
including this Airstream and a Shasta complete with her silvery wings.

People have dreams. Some chase their dreams, while others live them. They weave their love for vintage trailers into their lives. Whether it's having a little shop on wheels, owning a trailer park, or chasing the harvest across the heartland, they live life on their own terms. They have been given a gift—the gift of adventure. Here are their stories.

VICKIE

Meet Evelyn, as much of a head turner today as she was in 1954.

Strong women deserve to live on, either in our hearts and minds or memorialized in some unique way, like having a vintage trailer named after them. Vickie has merged her love of the strong women of her past with her love for vintage trailers and business. With Enchanted Trails, a village of trailer rentals, including seven vintage trailers, she has turned a plot of desert along Route 66 in Albuqueque, New Mexico, into an oasis for travelers.

Enchanted Trails welcomes weary travelers.

Vickie married into the Enchanted Trails family business more than twenty-nine years ago. As time passed, more and more family members left, including her ex-husband, until only she remained. Visitors can spend the night in a vintage trailer while experiencing New Mexico, the Land of Enchantment. She provides coffee and percolators (and even lessons on how to operate one), but doesn't allow cooking or showering in the trailers to preserve them. This is a special place for people to experience the past.

Like many trailer lovers, Vickie started out as a car aficionado and grew up riding in her dad's two-seaters. But the allure of a teardrop camper to tow behind those old cars had a definite appeal, so along came Alva, a 1956 teardrop. Her teardrop led to new desires, like the desire to get dressed while standing up, so the collecting began. To gain more room, she added Evelyn, a 1954 VaKaShunEtte. The Wisconsin gentleman who advertised it on eBay in 2004 wouldn't sell without the companion car, a '54 Ford Crestline. The trailer's frame was completely rotted, so a friend helped with the restoration and it turned out beautifully.

A VaKaShunette, Evelyn is quite the looker
with her 1950 Hudson Commodore tow vehicle.

· · · · · · · · · · · · · · · · · · · ·

She glows in the New Mexico sun.

Evelyn features a warm birch interior
and red accessories.

....

She has a cozy bed and well-appointed kitchen.

Flossie is a 1959 Spartan manufactured by the Spartan Aircraft Company. The company was founded in 1928 in Tulsa, Oklahoma, and closed in 1962.

Trailer after trailer followed, and Vickie's search for period accessories made her famous along back-road antique shops. Being known as "Trailer Lady" isn't such a bad thing when people start saving things they think might be the perfect fit. Her guest room is so filled with accessories, glassware, and textiles that she can shop in her own home.

Some people dream of living enchanted lives, but the lucky ones blaze their own trail to enchantment.

Guests are served on turquoise Melmac.

. . . .

You can practically smell the pot roast cooking
in this beautiful old oven, and no meal is complete
without a molded Jell-O salad.

Dot is a 1963 Winnebago
that was made for only two years.

. . . .

Della, a 1974 Silver Streak,
is a special breed, as no more than six were
produced in any week.

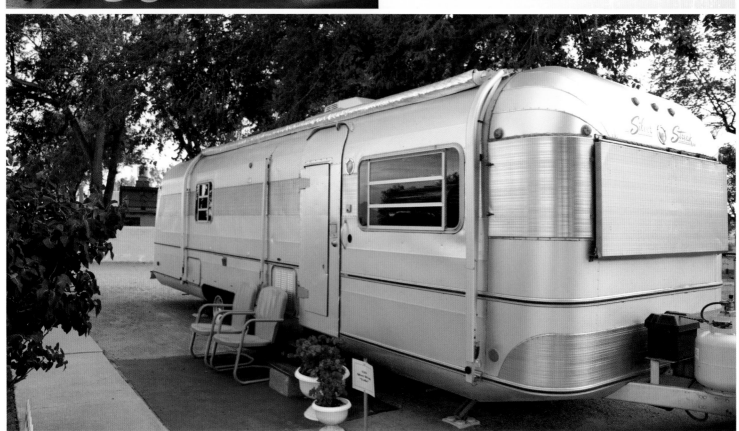

. . . .

The hippie-licious Josephine
is a 1969 Airstream parked at Enchanted Trails in
Albuquerque New Mexico.

....

Josephine's well-preserved cabinets have
tambour doors.

The interior of the Enchanted Trails Shasta
has a flamingo tea pot among her delightful accessories.

....

Barkcloth and chenille are the perfect pairing.

Yellowstone's slogan:
"Good on the go and great when you get there."

EMILY

As the sun dries the crops to a burnished gold, Emily chases the harvest, packing up her family and making it to the next state, the next town, and the next field before the storms come and take away a farm family's source of income for the year. She works all day and then travels long distances across the rural highways and back roads of the heartland. Over a period of twenty-five years, she has maintained a semblance of home for the young men who travel along in her family's aluminum mansion. Shoes are piled outside the door of her Spartan as she feeds the hungry crews, keeping them safe until she returns them to their mothers at the end of the harvest.

There have been good years and lean years, but custom harvesting is a way of life. Every year boys become men, and men teach the tough lessons of hard work, respect, and the integrity that go with the job. Hardships on the road teach you to appreciate farming and perseverance. Love of the land mixed with faith is what drives her forward. As one old harvest song says, "It takes a special kind of man to be a combine man. He's got to love the soil and want to see the land." That applies to the women of harvest as well.

Work boots are kicked off for supper served in an old Spartan trailer. Many a man-boy travels these circuits.

Working Spartans lined up for wheat harvest; not all vintage is for leisure.

. . . .

Laundry is just part of life when you chase the harvest across the plains.

SYLVIA

The icebox uses block ice to keep food cool.

"When you wish upon a star, makes no difference who you are, anything your heart desires will come to you ..." A shooting star represents a fleeting moment, but even as we close our eyes and make a wish, do we really believe it will come true?

Sylvia had one of those inimitable moments, so unexpected she still isn't quite sure why it crossed her mind. Her wish was to spend more time with her friend Larry, whom she had met at a trailer rally. Others saw the connection before they did, since both were fiercely concentrating on their own lives and families. But fate intervened, and like that shooting star, it was kismet.

Dreams are personal and sometimes all-encompassing and it is rare to find someone who shares it so completely, but Sylvia found that in Larry. Innocently meeting at a trailer rally, shared interests and an easy rapport is what started it all. A common dream is what ultimately cemented it: a vintage trailer park. Someplace to call their own, to showcase their trailers and let others enjoy them as much as they do. One shot, one chance to say "I gave it my best, with no regrets." While the perfect spot took four years to find, the name did not. The Starlite. Named for that shooting star, a logo was formed along with the vision, long before the property was found. The Starlite Classic Campground was born.

It is rare to find someone who shares your dream of operating a vintage trailer campground in which to showcase their treasures, but Sylvia found that person in Larry. The perfect campground spot took four years to find, but the name and logo were formed much earlier, along with the vision. The Starlite Classic Campground, named for that shooting star, was finally born in Canon City, Colorado.

The Flamingo lounge's dining area features refinished birch and flamingo fabrics.

Welcome to the Flamingo Lounge, a 1962 Tepee trailer hitched to a 1958 Chevy Biscayne.

The Spartan's signature wraparound windows brighten the living/dining room.

The trailers are loved and appreciated as intended, not rusting in backyards, gathering dust and intruders. They give other people a chance to sleep under chenille, experience solitude, and fantasize about what it was like to live in a different time and place.

On a hot, dry day in 2013, Larry and Sylvia's dream went up in smoke, literally. The nearby Royal Gorge Bridge & Park was consumed by a wildfire and everything in the 360-acre park except the historic 1929 bridge was destroyed. The year they were expecting to turn a corner on profits, there were suddenly no tourists, no campers, and no money to pay for expenses. Desperation, fear, and sadness rolled over them, but they didn't gave up. The park is open, the tourists are coming back, and the Starlite is once again filled with visitors. A dream that was meant to be shared; a love story; a shooting star—the same starlite that still shines in Larry's eyes when he talks about Sylvia.

Bailey, a Spartan Royal Mansion, is thirty-three feet long, weighs just over 6,000 pounds, and was built in the Tulsa plant in 1950. The previous owner purchased her in 1952 and raised three boys in the trailer. Bailey is truly a piece of travel trailer history.

. . . .

The warm, beautiful kitchen puts modern versions to shame.

An old Spartan sits in the tall grass,
sunning itself under mountain-blue skies.

....

Rear view of a 1957 New Moon
and a 1950 Spartan Royal Mansion.

Shaggy is a 1972 Ken-Craft with original fiberglass construction and oak interior.

··················

This 1957 New Moon has a full-size kitchen with metal cabinets.

Turquoise rules in vintage trailers.

....

The Starlite Classic Campground offers vintage trailer vacation rentals.

Meet Ginny, a 1954 Aljoa Sportsman parked at the
Starlite Classic Campground in Canon City, Colorado.

. . . .

With her vintage toaster,
Ginny is ready for breakfast guests and the smell
of Beech-Nut coffee wafts from the stove.

A 1959 Rambler station wagon is parked in front of a
1963 Shasta Airflyte.

....

The iconic flamingo. Wherever you find vintage trailers,
you will find a flock.

DAVE & LIZ

If you ever find yourself at a country fair, look for the Dawg House. "King Weiner" and his beautiful wife Liz are a fixture at fairs and festivals across the Rockies. They travel in their vintage 1966 Airstream and serve food out of the Dawg House, their shiny concession trailer. The food is simple and delicious, but they serve up more than great fare; they offer friendship and warmth wherever they go. Genuine is the one word that describes Dave & Liz best.

The work consists of long, hot days and late nights, and Dave's hunting trailer, a 1966 Airstream, is the perfect place to rest after a long day.

This modest old Airstream is used as a hunting cabin and retreat.

Chapter Eight

Oh, the possibilities

How do you end a book filled with possibilities? Whether you are a wizened collector or a voyeur peeking into the lives of these passionate collectors, the one thing collectors would want you to know is that the possibilities for owning a vintage trailer are endless. Travel with your eyes wide open and you will see little gems everywhere, forgotten and lonely, waiting for someone who cares enough to tow them home and give them a new life. Look in fields, alleys, junkyards, and backyards. Knock on doors. Take flowers and candy to little old ladies (with a wad of cash in your back pocket, just in case), and don't be afraid to admire the trailer and ask if it's for sale. Find others who share your passion. Just for fun, here are some possibilities for creating your own vintage trailer story.

A one-owner, 1959 Spartan Imperial Mansion sits empty in a rural town, waiting to be loved again.

Home for sale in Alma, Colorado, population 275.
At 10,578 feet, Alma is the highest incorporated town in North America and a beautiful place for a little retreat.

Peeking into yards, scouring alleys, and sometimes even looking along river beds is the best way to find these gems.

· · · · · · · · · · · · · · · · · · · ·

The search for the tow vehicle takes much the same path as the trailer search.

· · · · · · · · · · · · · · · · · · · ·

An old teardrop sits abandoned beside a pile of tires and badger carcasses.

. . . .

The aluminum sides of a 1949 Kamp Master have been replaced with wood (top left).

. . . .

Worn stripes gracing the softly weathered aluminum tell a story of travels long ago, possibly lumbering down Route 66 on family vacations.

Rust covers a forgotten hitch.

....

A 1957 Chevy, yet another tow vehicle waiting
to be restored (bottom left).

....

What might we find when we pop up this
vintage Minuteman (bottom right)?

Chinook spotted outside Anchorage, Alaska.
The family-owned company produced "The Sports Car of Motorhomes."

The purple shag carpet and VW front end on this sweet little rat rod makes the heart race!
Just a little minor body work and she is ready to roll. Proof that you never know what is sitting in backyards.

Chapter Nine

See you on down the road

When it comes to last words, vintage trailer lovers don't say goodbye, they say "see you on down the road," or maybe "happy trails." I look forward to seeing you again on the road, towing a sweet little vintage trailer, or driving a bus or van you love. One that gives peace and solace in a madly rushed world. One that provides joy and protects you when you need it most. See you on down the road.